FREE ROBUX

freebie.robloxiakid.com/r

Diary of a Roblox Noob:

The Great Jailbreak

Robloxia Kid

Contents

Chapter One:

Doing Hard Time

I woke up in the middle of the precinct. There were handcuffs on my wrists, and I was seated on a bench. There was a grumpy police officer in front of me. He sat behind a desk, and looked real busy. There were other policemen and they all looked just as busy and grumpy as that guy.

The entire precinct was a beehive of activity. The grumpy cops were escorting and taking a lot of other prisoners all around. The prisoners protested loudly and the other officers ignored them as they brought them to wherever they take prisoners. As you could imagine, the prisoners were not very happy with how they were being treated. Truth to tell, I wasn't very happy with where I was, either.

"What is this? Where am I, and why am I in these handcuffs?" I demanded.

Yeah, I was beginning to really sound just like the prisoners already. I was really going to fit into this place, really nice.

"That don't matter, Noob! You're here now, and you're going to do hard time!"

"What did you call me?" I asked.

"Noob! That's your name, and it suits you really fine, considering you're headed straight for the pen!"

The police officer that was handling me was the picture of friendliness and courtesy. It was clear that I was not going to get any answers from this guy. Still, I could not help but ask some important questions. I needed to get some idea of where I was, and what was going on.

"Hard time? Come on man, what was my crime?"

The police officer shrugged his shoulders and waved me away with his hand.

"What are you talking about? This is Roblox Jailbreak! In this server, you don't need no crime to be sent here to do hard time! Lucky for you, eh?"

That was a nice joke at my expense.

"I'm not serving any time for nothing!" I protested.

The police officer shook his head.

"If it's any consolation, most of these guys haven't done anything wrong either, but they're serving time all the same! Some of them though, actually have committed some kind of crime. I'm just not sure about your case."

"I don't even know how I got here! I just woke up with these chains on my wrists!" I said.

"Does it even matter? Look kid, the important thing now is, you're here, and you're doing time! So get up already, Noob!"

Yeah, it was a command and not a request. I had no other option but to get up from the bench. The policeman grabbed me by the arm and pulled me up.

"Come on, already! I've got a long day, and I want to go home to the wife and kids already. Let's go."

There was a slight hint of pity in the police officer's voice as I got up. It was there for a moment, but only for that moment. It passed quickly enough, and he frowned. I could see that this guy simply wanted to do his job, and that was that.

I really had no choice and simply followed the police officer. My hands were handcuffed, and he led me away from the noisy precinct.

Chapter Two:

A New Cellmate

I knew that he was not going to lead me anywhere better, and I was right. I passed through a metal detector that scanned my entire body. They made sure I wasn't carrying any custom parts that could start trouble in the prison.

"Okay. Dude's clear." the guard behind the metal detector said.

"His name's Noob." the police officer said.

"Heh. Noob. Suits him just fine."

"Never got to ask you your name, boss." I said.

The police officer smiled at me. ^"

"Boss will do just fine. Here."

Boss handed me a new set of clothes. At that moment, he was like some kind of magician. I never saw where he pulled those clothes from. It was almost like pulling several rabbits out of a hat, or something like that.

"Change into these. They look better on you."

It was a prison uniform. The color was a very plain and boring light brown. Well, I was really doing hard time now.

I had no choice but to change to the prison browns. Yep, I know what you're thinking. It was really tough to change clothes with my wrists handcuffed like that, but somehow, I managed. When I was done, I was looking really good.

Boss nodded and smiled at me.

"Yeah. You look good in prison browns, Noob." he said.

I frowned at him.

"Shut up, Boss."

It all happened so fast. I felt something hard and solid strike my tummy. It was a well-placed kick from Boss' boot, and let me tell you now, I really felt it. I thought that I would throw up, right then and there. Somehow, I managed to hold my breakfast in.

"You don't talk to me like that, ever. You got that, Noob?"

I shot a really angry look back at Boss. I guess I wasn't really thinking straight then. It was a bad move, for obvious reasons. After all, I wasn't the one with the power here.

Boss quickly made me pay for the dagger looks, as he struck me down with his baton. It looked like a plastic toy, but it really hit hard. I was knocked down, and the dude behind the metal detector just smiled and laughed it off.

"I said, did you get that, Noob?" he repeated.

"I got it loud and clear, Boss." I said.

"Good. Now let's get you back up on your feet. Come on, the boys are all dying to meet you, Noob."

I got up and started walking. Boss started walking beside me. Suddenly, he slipped hard on the floor. There was a loud thud as Boss fell right on his butt. Boss was a heavy sort, with a big belly to match. When he fell, the entire ground shook, and I thought that there was a minor earthquake. Well, seeing Boss fall flat on the ground, was too much, and I couldn't help but giggle just a little.

Boss immediately got up. With his heavy frame, and imposing presence it seemed as if it was his pride that was hurt more than anything. A guy that big and powerful could take on a tank head-on and still be standing. He dusted himself up and growled.

"What's so funny? Ain't never seen anyone slip before? Keep walking, already!"

I stopped laughing and continued walking, just as Boss said. I looked behind, and it became clear what happened. There was an errant banana peel that was right where Boss took a step. It was the culprit behind his very epic fail. I turned and saw the guard behind the metal detector. He smiled and winked at me. Boss never saw any of it.

I smiled back at the guard. I didn't know the guy at all, but it was clear that he didn't seem to like Boss very much. Well, I was happy to see Boss tripped up, in any kind of way. It was nice to know that not everybody liked Boss. Perhaps this would come in handy for me, later on.

Boss and I marched on, until we came to a large row of cells. There were several prisoners all around the cells, and there were as many as 5 floors all full of cells and prisoners.

"All right. We've got yard time in the afternoon where you can meet up and socialize with the other prisoners. You can do that if you're the friendly type. Personally, I wouldn't recommend it, though."

Yeah, it didn't take a genius to see that Boss was right. I immediately saw why he would not recommend me socializing with the other inmates. They were all in their cells, but they were all hooting and shouting all over the place. To say that they were noisy and rowdy was well, being mild. They were all acting like a bunch of caged monkeys.

"Are they always this noisy?" I asked.

Boss turned and smiled at me.

"Only when there's a new inmate town. Like now."

"Oh-kay."

A few more steps, and Boss led me to the second floor. I was led right smack into the cell in the middle of the cell block. There was a single inmate in the cell. There was also two beds stacked on top of each other in the cell. There was also a sink that was built into the wall. That was about it. Yeah, the cell was very well-furnished. I guess I couldn't complain. It wasn't like I was checking into a 5-star hotel with all the luxury in the world.

"Pablo! You've got a new cellmate!" Boss barked.

The other guy lifted his head up and smiled at me.

"Pablo Santana, ese. Nice to meet you."

Yeah, with that accent, and with the way he talked, he definitely sounded like a Pablo. Pablo was surprisingly very friendly and smiled at me, immediately. He offered me his hand, and he smiled. I could see that Pablo would be pretty easy to get along with. Well, that was definitely nice to see in a place like this.

I shook hands with Pablo, and my mood brightened, just a little bit.

"Nice to meet you, Pablo. I'm.."

"Noob. His name's Noob." Boss said.

I was a little relieved to hear Boss mention my name.

For some strange reason, I couldn't remember my real name, so I guess Noob it was, for now.

"Hi, Noob. Let's try to make our stay here, as pleasant as it can possibly be." Pablo said.

It was actually quite refreshing to see someone like Pablo in a place as depressing as this. Noob had a kind of positive energy that was actually quite easy to get as well. He kinda didn't fit in a prison like this, and I wondered what a nice guy like Pablo could have done to be in a place like this.

"Don't get too friendly with Pablo. You'll have to do a lot of hard time here, with him."

"A man's got a right to smile and enjoy himself, doesn't he?" I said.

Boss glared at me, as he approached me. Suddenly I felt like a rabbit being chased down by a large grizzly. Boss stood in front of me, and I could see just how large he really was. His big tummy only made him look even bigger and more intimidating.

"I've only met you now Noob, but already don't like you. Too bad for you. You better be nice here in the prison, because I'll be watching your every move." he said.

"Take it easy, Boss. I don't want any trouble. I just want to do my time."

Boss nodded, and turned away. He closed the cell door in front of me. It was just me and Pablo inside.

"Good. You better just keep it that way. For your sake."

Boss walked away, and this time, there were no banana peels in front of him. Eventually, even the other prisoners got quiet. I guess it was time to settle down in my cell with Pablo.

"Hey ese, what did you do to get on the Boss' bad side?" Pablo asked.

I shrugged my shoulder.

"Beats me. Boss was on my case the minute I stepped in here."

"That's too bad, ese. In case you hadn't noticed, he's the warden. Boss runs things around here, with an iron fist. If he doesn't like you, that's instant bad news for him."

I shook my head.

"It doesn't matter. After all, he won't be seeing me around here for long."

Pablo smiled and giggled at me.

"What do you mean, ese? Are you planning on getting out of here? Let me tell you now ese, lots of other guys have tried it before, and they all failed. You better just forget about any fancy ideas of escape. You'll just get burned, and make things worse."

I smiled and winked at Pablo.

"Is that so, now? Well, I say they call this server 'Jailbreak, right? I think it's time that we make it earn that name."

Chapter Three:

Something Loose

"Heh. I like your style, ese. You've got spunk, guts. All the stuff that makes for a tough guy. Too bad all of that doesn't amount to much down here. All it's going to do is make Boss angry, and you'll see soon enough, that he doesn't like getting angry."

Pablo spoke to me with caution, and I could see that he was very serious. It didn't matter to me, though. I was not going to spend time in jail for nothing. For me, the whole point of doing hard time was making amends for some kind of crime or bad stuff you did. Well, Boss simply couldn't pin anything on me, so there was no reason for me to stay locked up like this. I was determined to get out, one way or another. I just had to find out how to do it.

I immediately looked around the bare cell that I shared with Pablo. I observed all of our surroundings and took them all in very seriously. There wasn't much to look at. The walls were made of thick bricks and Roblox concrete, tough stuff to be sure. The only thing that passed for furnishing in the room was the sink. I immediately thought that perhaps there was a way to crack through it.

I went around it, and felt around the sink with my hands.

"Looking for weak spots in that sink, ese? I really wouldn't bother. It's wedged shut. The guards also do their rounds around here every hour, and they're always inspecting the cells, looking around for trouble. If you think we can dig through that sink, or somehow yank it out well, I just don't think it's possible."

I smiled at Pablo.

"Anything's possible, Pablo. We just have to make a plan, and follow through with it."

Pablo shrugged his shoulders.

"You're a different sort, all right, Noob. I just don't see how you can do it."

"We. It's we, Pablo. I can't break out of this place alone, papi. What do you say you help me, and we can both break out?"

Pablo's cheerful demeanor suddenly turned very serious. I could see the change in his mood, and it was almost instant.

"And get on the Boss' bad side? No way, ese! I don't want no trouble! I just want to do my time!"

"Doing your time, eh? Speaking of that, what are you here for anyway, and how long is your time in the prison supposed to be?"

"I got caught stealing some diamonds at the local jewelry store, ese."

Pablo's answer raised my eyebrows.

"Stealing diamonds, eh? Whatever for? You going to sell them somewhere?"

Pablo nodded.

"Yup. That's exactly what I wanted to do, ese. I wanted to steal them diamonds, but I didn't want to sell them."

"Really now? What were you going to do with them? Give them to someone special?"

When I mentioned someone special, Pablo's eyes lit up again. His cheerful mood came back almost instantly, and he was like a car that had just gotten a refill at the local station.

"Something like that, ese. It was for Maria and me."

"Maria? So you've got a special someone outside of the jail?"

Pablo nodded.

"Yup. Me and Maria we wanted to get out of the server. Those diamonds were our ticket out of here."

Okay. Now it was really getting interesting. I could

imagine Pablo giving those diamonds to someone special. Pablo looked like a really romantic sort, even if I didn't really care about such things. I just wanted to get out. What really got my attention was what he said. How could you possibly get out of the server with just diamonds?

"I think you lost me there with the 'getting out of the server part,' papi. How were you and Maria going to get out of the server with diamonds?"

Pablo began to speak a lot faster now. It was Pablo's habit to speak like a jackrabbit when he got excited. He was so excited that he piled the words all over each other. It was more than a little difficult to understand what he was saying.

"You haven't heard, ese? This server's gotten an upgrade, ese! An upgrade! That's big news! An upgrade! Do you what that means? I was the first one who discovered the upgrade, and now it's all over the news! It was that upgrade that was our ticket out of here!"

"Whoa, whoa. Slow down there, Pablo. I heard you the first time you mentioned the upgrade. You're liable to choke on your own words. Why don't you take it easy and explain this upgrade to me?"

Pablo did just that, and slowed down. He took some deep breaths, and finally began to make some sense.

"All right, ese. I get it. This is how it goes. There's a 'trains' upgrade to the server. Simply put, they'll be adding a whole slew of cool vehicles to the server. They're a lot of cool stuff that inmates like you and me, or anybody for that matter, never really got to using in the first version. They've got cars, a helicopter, a cool motorcycle, a snowmobile, and other stuff. It's the works, ese! But the best part is this."

"Go on. I'm listening."

"They've got trains too, ese!"

"Oh-kay. Trains are pretty cool, all by themselves, but I still don't see what that has to do with the diamonds that you stole."

Pablo put his hands together in an excited fist pump kind of thing. I clearly got him excited, and I already found Pablo to be quite a lovable character. At least hard time here wouldn't be so bad with Pablo around, right?

"Come on ese! Put two and two together! The whole trains upgrade thing is just the start. It's just the tip of the iceberg, so to speak. The trains, the new vehicles, they're all cool, but they're not telling you something. They're not telling everybody something. It's something only yours truly, Pablo Santana found out! All this, and I can speak Spanish too eh, ese? Estoy bien, genial!"

All this, and modesty too. Yup, that was good, old Pablo for you. A real character.

"So please, enlighten me, Pablo. What aren't they telling me?"

"The train has a supercar at the end, ese! It has a real badass engine, and can run by itself! The supercar is experimental, and it's powered by diamonds, ese! Maria is good with all this mech stuff, ese. She and I found out, and we realized we could escape the server! That's why I stole the diamonds in the first place. We were going to use it to power the supercar to break out of the server."

"Whoa, whoa, whoa! You're right, Pablo. This is big stuff. You're telling me this supercar can travel so fast it can break out of the server barrier? That's kind of like breaking through the barriers between servers. Science fiction stuff!"

"Time travel, faster than light, all that stuff. It's there in that supercar, ese. It can break out of the server. It's a big secret, and that's why they simply disguised the supercar as a simple piece of the train. The train runs around the prison, on its tracks. The entire facility was built around the prison ese. It would have been perfect."

Now it was me who was chuckling.

"Sounds to me like you took this escaping thing a lot more seriously than you first led on, Pablo." I said.

"You got that right, ese. Me and Maria, we wanted to get out of this server and start a new life together. That was until I got really sloppy, and the police caught me red-handed with the diamonds."

Pablo turned sad really quickly again. His shoulders hunched, and it seemed like a giant weight was placed on his shoulders. He really started to feel bad again.

"It would have been perfect but I got caught. Now I'm in prison, and Boss and the other guards won't

take their eyes off of me. It's hopeless ese, and it's all my fault."

I placed a hand on Pablo's shoulder, and smiled at him.

"There's always hope, Pablo. Cheer up. We will escape this place, and you'll get your new life with Maria. We'll both escape together."

I leaned on the sink, and as luck would have it, I immediately felt the sink budge. It moved, but ever so slightly. It was so slight, that you could barely notice it, but it was there. There was a weak point in the sink. My heart immediately jumped for joy inside of me.

"Did you feel that, Pablo?" I said.

Pablo shrugged his shoulders.

"Feel what, ese? You must be getting delirious or something."

"Look!"

I motioned his hand towards the sink. I grabbed it firmly with both hands, and so did Pablo. It shook, just a little bit.

"Did you feel that, Pablo? The sink is loose!" I said,

with excitement.

We both managed to make it budge, but it still wasn't strong enough to make any kind of a difference. The sink was still firmly attached to the wall, and it was impossible for me and Pablo to rip it off of its foundation. We simply weren't that strong.

"That's cool, ese. It really is, but I can't see where this is going. That sink is still wedged tightly on the wall. We're not dudes with superpowers. There's no way we're going to be able to yank it off."

"No, of course not. That still doesn't change the fact that it's loose, just a little bit. All we need to do is find something to pry it loose."

Pablo smiled at me.

"Something, or someone."

Chapter four:

Yard Time

It was my first time at the yard, and I intended to make the most of it. All the prisoners were outside at the prison yard, and for a few moments, we could soak in the sunshine and fresh air. It was quite refreshing to be out of our cells, but I wasn't here to take things easy or get lazy. No, I intended to make the most of yard time while I had it.

I looked outside the wire fence around us. The train tracks were right beside the prison, and the train

rumbled right beside us. The sound of the train was loud and booming. It sounded like some kind of angry dragon that was stretching its wings outside. Well, I was determined to ride that angry dragon out of the prison and to my freedom. I deserved as much, and so did Pablo.

The other inmates all did their thing around me and Pablo. Some of them lifted weights to keep in shape. Others played basketball at a nearby rusty goal and basket. A few others took in the sights like me. I wondered if they were planning some daring jailbreak like myself. Well, it didn't matter. The only thing that mattered for me now was getting out of there.

"All right, ese. You asked me yesterday for a way to yank that sink clean off. I've got that something for you, ese. Something, or more accurately, someone."

"Who is that someone, Pablo?"

Pablo pointed to one of the inmates lifting a large barbell above him. He was lying on a makeshift bench and doing some bench presses with it. The man was built like a tank, and he lifted the heavy weights with ease.

"That's Paquito over there, ese. Paquito Bonito's spent a lot of time here in jail ese. He was arrested by some cops when he was driving his van. The poor guy claims he's innocent, and I have to agree with him, ese. He says that he was just busy picking up his wife when they nabbed him. Poor Paquito was so big that five officers had to yank him out of his van."

"I can see what you mean about Paquito, Pablo. The guy is a powerhouse. What did they nab him for?"

"They arrested him for hit-and-run, ese. Story goes that Paquito was so caught up in picking up his wife on time that he ran over an elderly lady on the road. The poor old lady spent a lot of time at the hospital."

"Whoa. That's tough."

Pablo shook his head.

"You know what's tougher? Getting Paquito to even agree to all of this. The one person he's more terrified of than his wife is the Boss, ese! I don't know how you're going to convince him to help us. And even if you manage to do that, how are we possibly going to get him into our cell to do the deed?"

"I'll figure that out later, Pablo. First things, first. Let's talk to the big man."

We approached Paquito. He got bigger and bigger as we got nearer. I could see that the man wasn't built like a tank. He was built like 5 tanks. It was pretty obvious that Paquito wouldn't have a problem yanking that sink out of the wall. The only question now was, would he be willing to do it?

"Absolutely not, Pablo!"

Well, we got our answer right there. The words came right out of Paquito's mouth the moment we approached him.

"Come on, Paquito! If you yank that sink out of the wall, it will be easier for us to crawl through there, out of this prison!" I said.

"You look like a nice enough dude for a new inmate, Noob. I'm sure you mean well and all, but I can't see how this is going to work." Paquito said.

"If that thing is loose like you said, I won't have any trouble yanking it off. Heck, I probably wouldn't have any trouble yanking it off even if it was screwed on tight. All that being said, how do you know that we can crawl out of the prison from there?"

It was a valid question from the gentle giant, and I immediately had an answer for it.

"Our cell is located directly beside the tracks. Me and Pablo can hear the trains roaring beside us. If you yank that sink from the wall it will punch a hole through it. From that hole, we can make it to the train, and freedom."

Paquito shook his head and retreated from us. It was kinda funny watching a huge man like that retreating like a little mouse in fear. It was both funny and scary. It got scary when he explained why he was so frightened.

"So you guys want me to get inside your cell and yank that sink off? No way. Nope. No! It's just out of the question."

"Take it easy, big guy. Why are you so scared of doing it, anyway?" I asked.

"The Boss. If he finds out about it, he's going to have my head! If he even knew what we were planning, we would really get it for sure!"

There it was again, or more accurately, there he was again. It was the Boss. Pablo was afraid of him, but Paquito was simply shaking in his boots at the mere mention of the Boss' name. I began to wonder what kind of a man was Boss to have such a hold on all these men? These were hardened criminals, men who should have not been afraid of anything. They were not afraid of anything, except the Boss. What kind of a man could command such fear and respect? I didn't know the answer to that question. All I knew was that this Boss was really something of a terror in the jail.

"Look, Paquito. Come on now! This maximum security prison isn't what it really is, you know. It's got a real weak point, and me and Pablo here, are literally sitting on it! We just need your strength to knock that sink out of the wall, and we're free! Don't you want to be free? Come on!"

I saw a look of hope come over Paquito's eyes. There was real hope and a fire that wasn't there before. I really saw something and it was just a matter of fanning those flames so it could get Paquito to move. Unfortunately, that moment lasted much too soon. The flames were there, and were gone again. The moment simply came and went, just like that.

"I do. I really do. I'm just too afraid of the Boss to try and escape like that."

"Come on now, big guy! If you don't overcome that fear, you'll stay in prison here. We all will! You've got to.."

"All right! Yard time's over! Everybody back to their cells!"

The loud and booming voice of the Boss came over a loudspeaker. He was announcing the end of yard time. The other guards were already moving to get us all back into our cells.

"All right, Pablo. Paquito. Noob. You guys heard the Boss. Your friendly chit-chat time is up. Let's break it up and get going."

The guard moved us all back to our cells, and there was really nothing we could do. We just went back like quiet sheep. You couldn't really blame us, and you couldn't really blame Paquito too, I guess. I was asking him to take something of a leap of faith. That wasn't easy for anyone.

The guard led me and Pablo back to our cell. He silently slid our door closed. The bars were between us and the cell block again.

"Well, it was a nice try, Noob. I'll give you that. You tried to talk the big man into going with our plan, but he just backed out. Nothing you can do about that, and there's no shame in it. You did your best."

I shook my head. Yeah, I was frustrated over the results of our talk with Paquito. I wasn't completely out of hope though.

"It's never over until it really is over, Pablo. Something tells me that Paquito will come around sooner or later. When that happens, we'll have our chance to get out of here."

As it turned out, that chance came a lot sooner than I expected.

Chapter Five:

The Choice

"What do you mean I have to build a new wall in 3 days?"

We all overheard Paquito arguing with the Boss. His voice was loud enough so that everyone in the yard heard what they were all talking about. Paquito did not even bother to hide the frustration in his voice. This was just my 8th time at the yard. I had spent around a week in prison.

"Come on, Paquito. You know you're the strongest one here in the prison. No one can match your strength. That's why I need you for the job. You're the only one who can do the job right." the Boss said.

"I know what you need me for Boss, but what you're asking me to do is just plain unfair. You're asking me to do the job of ten men in half the time! Even my strength has its limits!"

Paquito was protesting really hard, but the Boss would not be swayed. There was a reason why he was t

jail's warden, and known as the Boss.

"You know Paquito, I've been asking you nicely all this time. However, you're a pretty stubborn fellow, and my patience has its limits."

"What do you mean, Boss?"

The Boss looked Paquito in the eye. There was no hint of fear in his entire body. Most men would be terrified of such a giant man like Paquito, but not the Boss. He simply stared him down, and did not budge from where he was standing.

"I tried to be nice and polite to you, Paquito. I just didn't want to hurt your feelings or anything, but that doesn't mean that I'll go soft on you. If asking you nicely won't do the trick, I'll simply have to force you to do it."

"What? I don't understand."

"Understand this! If you don't do the work and complete that new wall in three days, I'll make sure you spend the rest of your sentence in solitary confinement!"

Paquito trembled at the sound of solitary confinement. It was every prisoner's worst nightmare. No one wanted to go into solitary confinement, and for good reason.

"All right already! I'll do it!"

The warden smiled when he heard Paquito agree to building the large wall. He smiled and looked very pleased with himself. I also smiled at Pablo.

"There you go. I knew you were a reasonable dude, Paquito. You can start working immediately."

"All right Boss."

The Boss left Paquito feeling very miserable, while he felt like a winner in every sense. Well, the Boss was definitely a bully in the yard. Paquito was anything but enthusiastic when he answered the Boss. It was clear that he was anything but happy to work on that wall. That was a good thing for us, and the chance that we had been waiting for.

"You heard that, Pablo?" I asked.

"How could I not? They didn't even bother to keep their conversation to themselves, ese."

"Well, remember how you were asking me how we could possibly convince Paquito to help us? I think we've just found our way."

I sounded really pleased and very hopeful, but Pablo did not share my good vibes. He still had his doubts about everything.

"I still don't see how we can use any of that to our advantage, ese. Paquito still doesn't look pretty helpful."

"You leave the convincing to me. Just tell me now. How much time do we have before yard time ends?"

"I think we still have some time."

That was the answer that I was waiting to hear.

"Great. Come with me, but let me do all the talking."

Pablo shrugged his shoulders.

"All right, ese. It's your call. You're the man with the plan."

I approached Paquito with full confidence. The Boss was long gone, and he was also very confident that he had a good worker with Paquito.

"Hey, Paquito. I overheard you and the Boss talking about that wall you're going to make."

"Hey Noob. Pablo. I guess everybody in the yard heard us talking. I can't believe what he's asking me to do, but I've got no choice. If I don't do it, I'll be stuck in solitary! You know what that's like? It's terrible!"

"I gotta admit big guy, I don't. That's because I've just been here at the prison for less than a month. I don't know what it's like, and frankly, I don't want to know."

"It's terrible, man! You're just sitting there all alone and.."

"Get it together, Paquito! I didn't come here to compare notes about solitary. I came here to remind you about my offer again."

"The breakout thing? Again? Come on, Noob! I already told you that I'm not interested and.."

"Listen here, Paquito. The Boss is a bully, plain and simple. I know how bullies are, and take it from me, he's not going to change. You finish this wall for him, and you avoid solitary, that's great. It really is. However, it's not going to end there. The Boss has seen that you're a strong guy, and he's going to keep taking advantage of that strength, over and over again. That's simply how bullies are. This wall won't be the end of it. There will be a lot of other stuff in the future, and you won't be able to say no. You can keep taking all that from the Boss, or you can choose to end it, by breaking out with us."

For a moment, we all didn't say anything. The three of us just looked at each other, and I could see that the big guy was really thinking about what I said.

"It's your choice, ese." Pablo said.

Finally, Paquito spoke up.

"That's a great offer guys, but I still can't do it. I'm sorry."

Chapter Six:

The Plan

I didn't hear the end of it from Pablo after that. It got so bad that he just kept ranting about my epic fail, night after night. Worse than that, I even heard it during the day.

"Well, that was a nice speech and all, ese! It really moved the big guy, and gave us the results we wanted, eh? What did I tell you, ese? I told you that big ox was an idiot! I told you we're trapped here in this prison. We might as well accept it. It will be a lot easier for all of us, that way."

Pablo spoke his mind, and there was really nothing that I could say. He was right. I seemed to have expected too much out of Paquito. Pablo ranted like that, over and over again, night after night. Yeah, I really lost a lot of sleep because of Pablo's disappointment.

"Ok, ok! I get it, papi! I really do! You've been ranting about this for 3 days and nights, Pablo. Give it a rest already."

I was literally covering my face with my arms now. It had been the third day since the Boss spoke with Paquito. The wall had almost been done now, and we were outside at the yard. Pablo would not let me hear the end of it.

"Yeah, you heard me right, ese! Sure sucks, doesn't it, ese? I told you to stop filling our heads with hope and all that stuff! We're just going to stay here and rot! It's awful, ese!"

Pablo was starting to sound as if he was angrier at himself than he was at me.

"Are you done, Pablo? It's been three days already, and you've done nothing but rant over and over again about Paquito and the yard!"

"I'm sorry, ese. I really am. I guess I just thought the big ox was better than that. I thought that he would actually well, help us, you know?"

Yeah, so he was angrier at himself than he was at me. More accurately, I guess he was more angry at Paquito for not helping us.

"Look, I feel you bro. I really do. I gave him a great offer and he refused. There's really nothing we can do about it. We just have to move on and."

A huge and imposing figure approached us. We immediately recognized him as Paquito.

"Hi guys." the big man said.

The Great Jailbreak

The big man looked sad and very down. Well, I guess that was usually the case with Paquito, so there was no surprise there. The big surprise however, was Pablo suddenly blowing up all over him. I thought he had gotten tired of ranting for 3 straight days and nights. Apparently, not.

"Hi yourself, ese! How's that wall of yours coming, ese? We gave you a chance to help us escape! A genuine chance to escape, and you blew us off! I hope you're happy with yourself!"

"That's just it, Pablo. I just wanted to say that.."

"Say what? That we suck and you rock because you made that wall? I really hope you're happy with yourself, Paquito! I mean, for a guy as big and strong as you are, you really lack brains! You should have helped us!"

"Pablo.."

I tried to calm him down, but there was no getting to Pablo. Yeah that was Pablo for you. The guy was lovable and all, but he had a temper too, and he didn't like being pushed around or rejected like that.

"No! This guy's got a lot of nerve coming back to us, Noob! After what he did.."

"Pablo, let's let the man speak, shall we?"

Somehow, I got him to shut up for a few moments, and Paquito finally did speak. He spoke plainly, and straight to the point.

"Guys, I'm in."

When I heard Paquito, I was surprised, and I felt awesome! Finally, the big man came to his senses! Super cool!

"Whoa. Did I get my hearing straight? Did I just hear what I heard? Did you just say that.."

Pablo's jaw dropped, and he was at a loss for words. I guess I couldn't blame him.

"Yeah. You heard me right. I'm in. I'll help you guys break out."

"I gotta ask man. Why the change of heart all of a sudden?" I asked.

Paquito answered with a frown on his face. Something obviously went wrong here.

"I'm about to finish the wall and all, but the Boss is still getting on my case. He says once I'm done here, I'm supposed to construct a new wing for the prison in 3 days more. A new wing! Can you believe that? He's turning me into his one man construction crew! And at no extra cost! That ain't fair at all!"

"What did we tell you, ese? Boss will just take advantage of you."

"That doesn't matter anymore, Pablo. What matters now is that he's on our side. Time to break out of here."

"Great! Great! We're getting outta here!"

Pablo was so happy that Paquito finally accepted and he could hardly contain his excitement. The big man knew exactly what I was thinking, and he silently agreed. He placed one of his giant hands on Pablo's mouth. Pablo was always a very emotional and passionate person. Many times he was just too much.

"Go ahead and shout little louder ese! I guess you want everyone else to know what you're planning! With a little luck, you'll reveal the entire thing to the Boss and we'll be done before we even start!" I said.

"Noob's right! We were just lucky that no one heard you shouting like that because there's a pickup game there of b.ball that everyone's betting on!" Paquito said.

The big guy was a lot smarter than he looked.

Pablo silently nodded. When we could see that he would keep his mouth shut, Paquito finally let go.

"Sorry guys. Don't know what came over me. I can get a little carried away, eh?"

"Well keep it together, ese! I can't do anything if everyone finds out about this plan before it even happens!"

"Uh, Noob? Speaking of keeping it together, I was just wondering right now.

It was Paquito. He had something on his mind.

"Yeah?"

"Just how are we going to break out? Like I said earlier, I can't just waltz in your cell and yank that sink loose."

I smiled at them both.

"I've already got that covered. You see, I've got a plan."

Chapter Seven:

The Big Swing

A plan is the most important thing to have anytime, and anywhere. If there's anything that I learned, it's that you've always got to have a plan. A plan is the most important thing to have, if you have any kind of problem. See, the plan's like a map. Your solution to the problem is the destination you want to go. The problem itself is the whole wide unfamiliar land. It's full of obstacles and strange stuff. A plan gives you direction and a clear means to get to your destination. Without the plan? You might as well be a lost babe in the woods.

Like I said earlier to Paquito in the yard, I had a plan, and it was time to execute it.

The Boss' loud voice came through the speakers.

"All right, losers! Time for roll call!"

Roll call was when all of the prisoners left their cells and stayed inside the cell block. A head count was made to make sure all the prisoners were still around the prison. Kind of like attendance in school. Well, attendance was the perfect time to make a break for it.

The guards all slid us out of our cells and we all stood at the center of the prison area. There we were, several of us all standing there as a few guards, and the Boss himself, counted us off.

Pablo stood beside me nervously. He could barely stand still and stay calm through it all.

"The guards are counting off, ese. You think he'll do it, ese?"

"Calm down, Pablo. Have a little faith in Paquito. I'm sure he'll come through." I said.

The Boss called out everyone's name, and you had to answer with a loud and resounding 'Present!' That was how roll call went, and so far, Paquito had not made his move yet.

"A2K!"

"Present!"

"Big Stimpza!"

"Present!"

"Da Shiek Ha!"

"Present!"

As you can see, roll call could take more than a

while to get done. There were so many of us, and we would all be called out one-by-one. Well, Paquito would simply not wait that long.

Before any other names were rattled off, the big guy made his move, just as we planned. I saw it all come down.

Paquito socked the nearest prisoner beside him. The impact of his fist knocked the poor guy out. Once he was out, Paquito did something, only someone with his strength could do. He picked up the poor guy on his ankles, and began to swing him around like a baseball bat. I think they call that move a 'big swing' in Pro Wrestling, but I'm getting ahead of myself here.

As you can imagine, Paquito's wrestling move knocked down several prisoners, and immediately caused mayhem. Chaos and craziness erupted everywhere, and all the prisoners were immediately riled up. Several of them started to try and beat up Paquito.

He was more than capable of fending them off. With one swing of his fist, he knocked down three of them. A few other prisoners came to his defense.

"What is that moron Paquito trying to do? Order! Let's get some order around here!" the Boss said.

The guards all jumped into the chaos, but they were only a few men. They were soon overwhelmed by the sheer number of the prisoners. Everyone was knocking, punching, or kicking someone else, and order was simply impossible, at least for the moment.

I socked one prisoner in front of me.

"Come on, Pablo! That's our cue! It's time to head back to our cell!" I said.

"What about Paquito? We won't be able to yank out the sink ourselves!"

"You called?"

It was Paquito, and he was standing in front of us smiling. He had bulldozed through several guards and prisoners and was now standing in front of us.

"Come on! This madness won't last forever!"

We made a break up the now empty cell blocks. We reached our cell, and like the others, it was open. The cell doors had all slid open for roll call, and we easily got in. I pointed at the sink.

"There's the sink, Paquito! You think you can.."

"Done."

Paquito didn't even let me finish my sentence. Before I could finish, he simply yanked the sink from the wall. He yanked it as easily as someone would slide a drawer open from a desk. It came off with a large chunk of the wall. His strength was amazing.

When he was done, there was a large hole the size of Paquito. It was a hole that would fit all of us, considering me and Pablo were much smaller than

Paquito.

"Well. He's efficient, isn't he?" Pablo said.

Paquito grinned at us. He was very proud of the damage he had caused.

"Like taking candy from a baby!" he said.

"All right, you two. No time to pat everyone on the back. We can do that when we're outside." I said.

The gust of wind outside and the sounds of the city blasted us from the outside. The train tracks were literally right beside our cell! Everything was working, just as I had planned.

It was then that we realized just how close we were to escaping the prison. For a moment, we were all struck by what was just happening. We couldn't help but savor the moment. We were so close to freedom now!

"Do you hear that? Do you feel that? It's everything outside! We're free!" Pablo said.

We all felt really good, but I wasn't kidding when I said that there wasn't much time to pat everyone on the back.

"Hey! What are you three up to?"

We looked down from our cell and saw Boss. He had seen what we had done, and was already moving up the steps towards us. The commotion was already dying down, and several guards were already taking the place of the ones who had been struck down in all the chaos. I had to hand it to him. The Boss really had this prison under his strict control.

"It's the Boss! He's on to us! We've got to get moving!" I said.

"No kidding!"

The roar of the train from the outside sounded, and we all heard it. The cell shook all around us, as the train approached.

"It's coming! I hope Maria will do her part of the plan!" I said.

Pablo smiled at me.

"Have a little faith in my mami, ese! She will come through on this!"

Pablo smiled at me from ear-to-ear. With a smile like that, how could I not doubt him? Right as he smiled, the rumbling and the shaking got louder and louder.

"You hear that? It's the train! It's coming right on schedule! I told you my Mami would come through for us! She always does!"

I was very happy to see that Pablo had so much faith in Maria. With the train rumbling closer towards us, it was hard not to have faith in her.

"It's coming!" Pablo said.

"That's great and all, but it's got to slow down for us to jump inside!" I said.

"Have a little faith, ese!"

The rumbling and the shaking began to get weaker. I felt the floor under us go stable again. It could only mean one thing; the train was slowing down!

"The train's slowing down! How is that even possible?" Paquito said.

"Noob and I planned this all out! When you agreed to break open the wall through the sink, we already told Maria to board the train, and somehow slow it down!"

"She did that?" Paquito said.

Pablo shrugged his shoulders.

"Hey, that's my mami for you, ese!"

The train rumbled on, and it finally began to approach our cell. Within a few moments, the train came into sight. It was huge and painted bright orange. The giant train was an amazing sight to see, especially for prisoners like us.

"It's right there in front of us!" Paquito said.

The train was now moving at a snail's pace. It would be a lot easier for us to jump onto the train from where we were because of its decreased speed. Only a few things needed to be fixed now.

"Come on, come on!" I said.

"Hold it right there, you are crazy cons!"

"Oh no! Not now!"

It was the Boss. He had managed to enter the cell along with several guards behind him. Yeah, his timing could not have been worse.

"No! Not now! Not when we're so close!" I said.

"Not a problem!"

Paquito moved towards them and punched the Boss flush on the face. The Boss went flying back, knocking his men over. They were down on the ground but they would not stay down for long.

The car that we had been waiting for, was now almost in front of us. It was the supercar that Pablo had told us about. It was right in front of the cell and its door was open. There was a nice lady waving in the car.

"Mami!"

"Pablo! You and your friends must jump in now!" she said.

"Go! Go!"

Pablo went first. He took a huge leap of faith, and managed to land in the car. I looked back and saw Paquito was still busy fighting off the guards.

"Paquito! Come on!" I said.

"Go already! I'll hold them off!"

I didn't like it, but I had no choice. I jumped, and

landed on the supercar's floor. It was definitely a rough landing, but I was inside.

The train was already gaining speed. I got up and saw Paquito take the final leap. Just as I stood up, he leaped right at me. He landed on top of me. The impact was incredible. It was like getting hit by the train. My breath was knocked out of me.

"Noob!"

"Noob man, I'm sorry! Are you all right?"

I looked up, and saw Paquito sitting on top of me.

"I will be once you get off me!"

"Oops, sorry!"

He got off me, and my breath rushed back just in time. I thought I would get choked, but I managed.

"Guys, this is Maria. Maria, this is Paquito and Noob, my friends from the prison."

Maria smiled at me and Paquito. I was happy to meet her, and even happier that she and Pablo were back together. Well, it was all's well that ends well, right? Not really.

"Guys, we've got trouble! Look!"

Paquito pointed out the supercar's window. There was a large helicopter flying above us. I could make out Boss sitting inside beside the pilot.

"Stop this train now! There are escaped felons

inside!" he said, over the helicopter's loudspeaker.

Yeah, there was more trouble.

Chapter Eight:

The Big Explosion

"All right, Pablo. We've gotten this far because of your knowledge about this secret supercar. Now we'll really see if it's all that it was hyped up to be!" I said.

Pablo nodded.

"Don't worry Noob! I studied all about this car and what it can do. Look!"

Pablo pressed a button on the car's wall. The car shook violently, and we were all knocked to the ground. There was a powerful heave, and it felt like the supercar was breaking away from the train. With one powerful heave, it did just that.

I looked out the window and my eyes almost popped out. There were clouds and the blue sky all around us.

"Whoa! It's flying!" I said.

"How is this even possible?" Paquito said.

"I told you guys! This supercar's an experimental prototype that can do all sorts of cool things! Once it gains momentum, it can blast us out of the very server!"

It probably would have done just that, but it was not meant to be. We felt powerful gunfire hammer the supercar's walls. We all knew what it was. It was the police helicopter, and it was opening fire on the supercar.

"They're shooting at us!" I said.

The supercar took heavy damage from all that gunfire. There was no way that it was going to stay in the air with such an assault. The supercar shook violently, and we felt the air rushing all around us.

"We're going to crash! Everyone hold tight!"

Paquito held onto one of the car's railings, Pablo embraced Maria, and I just tried to stay standing. This would be a violent landing, one way or another.

The supercar crashed to the ground with terrible intensity. We felt the ground hit the car, and we were all thrown and knocked about the supercar. It was simply not possible to stay standing, as it hit the ground.

The supercar skidded and rocked the ground as it was out of control. We were bounced around inside, and I thought that the supercar would never stop.

The Great Jailbreak

Somehow, it did.

We were all on the floor, as the supercar finally stopped skidding. The windows were all smashed, and there were several dents on the walls around us. There was also some smoke coming from somewhere. The supercar was a total wreck.

"Everybody all right?" I asked.

I looked around. Paquito, Maria, and Pablo were all still in one piece. They were pretty banged up, yeah that was for sure, but at least everyone was okay.

"That was the roughest landing ever! Even I can't take a pounding like that again." Paquito said.

"The supercar's trashed! We have to get out!" Pablo said.

We all left the car, and stepped out into thick woods. There was a trail of fallen trees and burnt ground where the supercar crashed. It was still smoking behind us.

"Go! Go!"

After we had run a considerable distance, there was a powerful explosion. The supercar blew up in a ball of fire. Thankfully, none of us were inside.

"Whoa! That was one heck of an explosion! The boss is sure to see that!" Paquito said.

I smiled at the three of them.

"That is all to our advantage." I said.

Pablo looked at me with wide eyes that did not understand anything that I had just said.

"Did I just hear you right, ese? How can any of this be for our good? The supercar's completely destroyed and we can't escape to another server!" he said.

Good point. I was still smiling.

"I know all that. But it's still okay. That's because the explosion has guaranteed our freedom. The Boss should believe now that we all kicked the bucket with that blast, and for good reason. No one could have survived a blast like that, right?"

We all looked up and saw the police helicopter. It was already flying away from the scene of the explosion. I smiled at everyone.

"We may not have escaped this server, but we definitely broke out of the prison, and we're free!" I said.

"We, we did it. Didn't we?"

Pablo and the others couldn't believe it, but I was right. Our freedom was right there in front of us.

"Give me some skin guys!"

High-fives were exchanged all around. Everyone was happy and in good spirits. We had escaped the prison and the Boss thought that we were all done for. Everything ended up pretty good, don't you think?

The Great Jailbreak

It was a long walk out of the woods to the next town, but none of us really minded any of that. After all, we were free. A whole new life and maybe a new set of adventures awaited us all. Anything was possible now that we were out of jail.

The End!

Thanks so much for reading this book!

If you like my work, search for and follow Robloxia Kid on Facebook AND Amazon to get access to my free short stories, special giveaways, new books and more:

Also, tune in to my awesome website:

robloxiakid.com

If you figured it out, email me at
inforobloxiakid@gmail.com :)

If you enjoyed this book, please leave a review on
Amazon! It would really help me with the series.

Best,

Robloxia Kid

Made in the USA
Middletown, DE
13 August 2018